Bab

1 2 3

1

2 3

Brown Watson

ENGLAND

1 teddy

2 dogs

3 cars

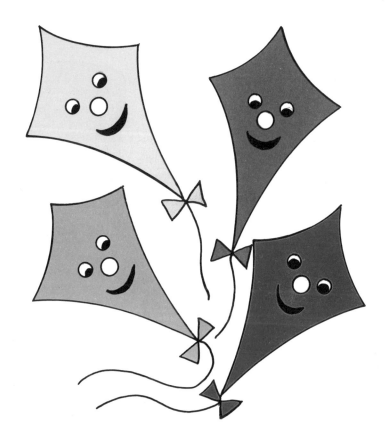

4 kites

5 drums

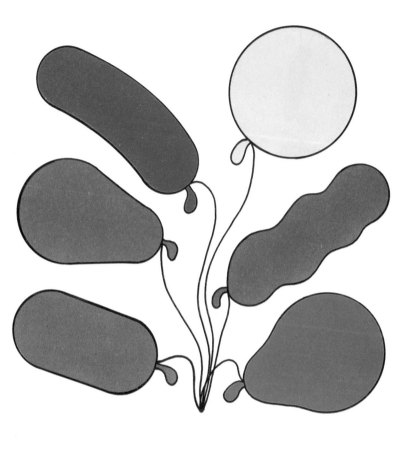

6 balloons

7 butterflies

8 engines

9 flowers

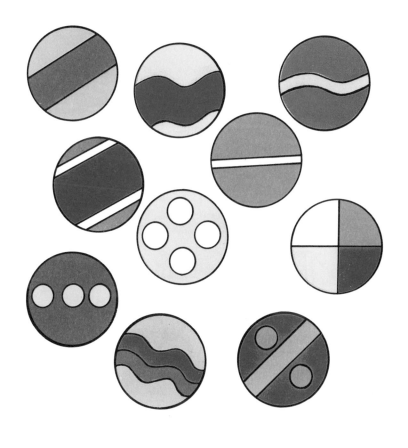

10 balls

How many boats can you see?

How many books can you see?

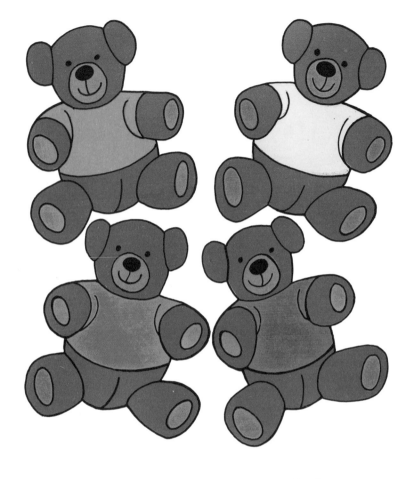

How many teddies can you see?

How many keys can you see?

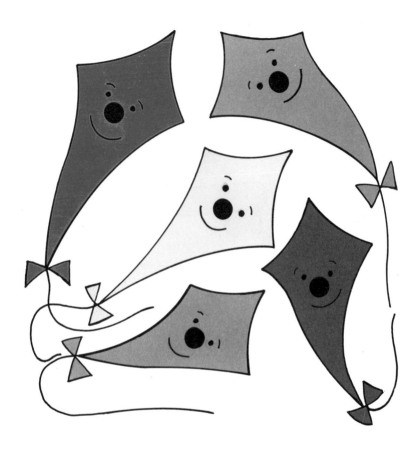

How many blue
kites can you see?

How many houses can you see?

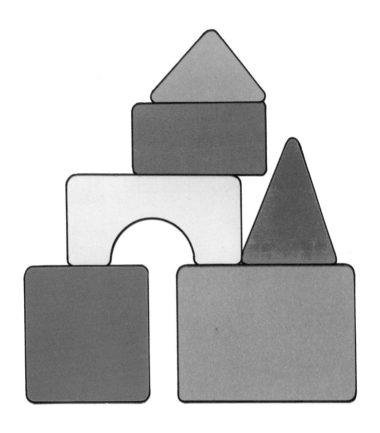

How many red bricks can you see?

How many buckets can you see?

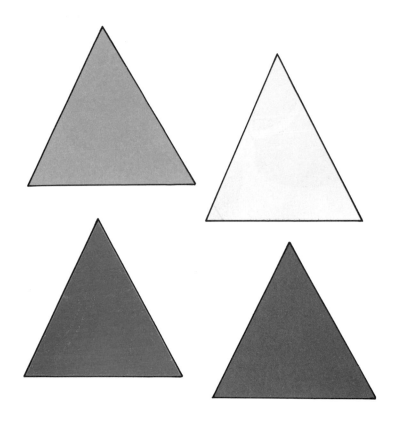

How many triangles can you see?

How many squares can you see?

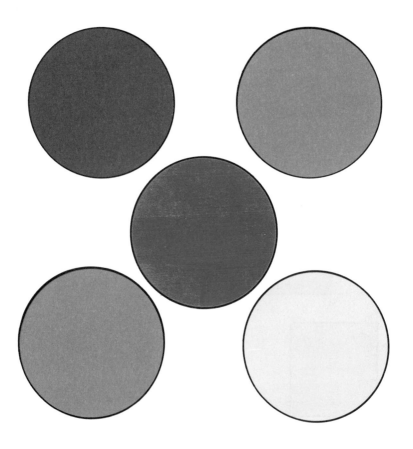

How many circles can you see?

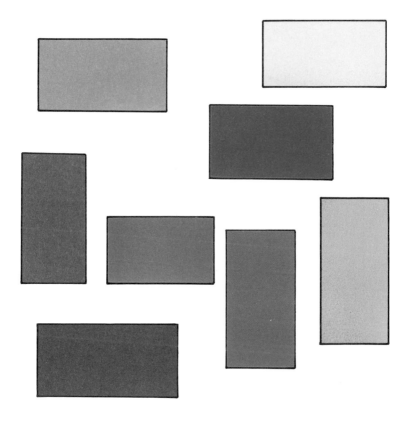

How many rectangles can you see?

The table has four legs.

The ladybird has
six legs.

The cat has
two ears.

How many pairs of shoes can you see?

Which gloves are the same?